DEGREES OF DESPAIR

THE STRUGGLE OF SOUTH AFRICA'S EDUCATED UNEMPLOYED YOUTH

MICHAEL MOKOBANE

First Edition 2024

Published by Michael Mokobane

Introduction

South Africa's educated youth are facing a crisis of unprecedented proportions. Despite possessing the skills and qualifications necessary to succeed, hundreds of thousands of young people are struggling to find employment. This phenomenon has far-reaching consequences, not only for the individuals affected but also for the country's economic and social fabric.

The statistics are alarming:

- Over 50% of South African youth are unemployed

- 60% of graduates are unemployed six months after graduation

- The youth unemployment rate is three times higher than the national average

Personal Stories of Struggle and Despair

Meet Njabulo, a 25-year-old graduate with a degree in engineering. Despite applying to numerous job openings, he remains unemployed, forced to live with his parents and rely on their financial support. His story is not unique; many of his peers share similar experiences.

Or consider the case of Thandi, a 28-year-old with a master's degree in business administration. After months of searching, she finally secured a low-paying internship, only to be retrenched a few months later. Her confidence shattered, she now doubts her ability to succeed in the job market.

These stories illustrate the desperation and hopelessness that pervade the lives of many educated young South Africans. The promise of education, once seen as a ticket to success, now seems like a distant dream.

Purpose of the Book

This book aims to explore the complex issues surrounding the high unemployment rates among educated South African youth. Through a combination of research, and personal stories, we will examine the causes, consequences, and potential solutions to this crisis.

By shedding light on the struggles faced by Njabulo, Thandi, and countless others, we hope to spark a national conversation about the need for urgent action. It is only by working together that we can create a brighter future for South Africa's educated unemployed youth.

Key Questions to be explored:

- What are the root causes of high unemployment among educated youth in South Africa?

- How do social, economic, and political factors contribute to this crisis?

- What are the emotional and psychological consequences of prolonged unemployment for young people?

- What potential solutions can be implemented to address this issue, and what role can government, education institutions, and individuals play?

Contents

Chapter 1: The Education System   1

Chapter 2: The Job Market   10

Chapter 3: The Struggle is Real   18

Chapter 4: Societal Expectations   26

Chapter 5: Government Initiatives   34

Chapter 6: Entrepreneurship and Innovation   44

Chapter 7: Breaking the Cycle   53

Chapter 8: The Path Forward   62

Can I Ask A Favour?   69

CHAPTER 1: THE EDUCATION SYSTEM

South Africa's education system is a cornerstone of the nation's development and a key driver for social and economic progress. However, it is also one of the most complex and troubled sectors in the country. Despite substantial reforms and investments since the end of apartheid, the system continues to face significant challenges that undermine its effectiveness, particularly in preparing graduates for the job market. This chapter provides a detailed overview of South Africa's education system, identifies the key challenges it faces, and explores the impact of these challenges on graduate employability.

Overview of South Africa's Education System

South Africa's education system is structured into several key stages:

- **Primary and Secondary Education:** Comprising 12 years of schooling, from Grade 1 to Grade 12.

The primary and secondary education system is overseen by the Department of Basic Education (DBE), which is responsible for setting curriculum standards, managing public schools, and ensuring that all children have access to basic education.

- **Tertiary Education:** Includes universities, universities of technology, and technical and vocational education and training (TVET) colleges. The Department of Higher Education and Training (DHET) governs this sector, which offers a range of academic and vocational programs designed to equip students with the knowledge and skills necessary for various careers.

- **Vocational Training and Skills Development Programs:** These programs aim to provide practical skills and training in specific trades or professions. They are particularly important for students who do not pursue traditional academic pathways but still require qualifications that can lead to employment.

Despite this well-structured system, the reality on the ground is far from ideal. The system is characterized by disparities in quality and access, with many students, particularly those from disadvantaged backgrounds, facing significant barriers to obtaining a quality education.

Challenges Facing the Education System

Despite the progress made in expanding access to education since the apartheid era, South Africa's education system continues to grapple with several critical challenges that impede its effectiveness.

1. **Inadequate Funding**

Funding remains one of the most pressing issues facing South Africa's education system. While the government allocates a significant portion of its budget to education, the resources are often insufficient to meet the growing demands of a rapidly expanding student population. This inadequacy is particularly evident in the public school system, where limited funding leads to:

- **Resource Shortages:** Schools struggle to provide basic resources such as textbooks, learning materials, and adequate facilities. This shortage severely hampers the quality of education, particularly in rural and under-resourced urban areas.

- **Underpaid and Undervalued Teachers:** Budget constraints often mean that teachers are underpaid and lack access to ongoing professional development. This not only affects their morale but also limits their ability to deliver high-quality education.

2. **Poor Infrastructure**

Infrastructure is another significant challenge, with many schools across the country suffering from inadequate facilities. This includes:

- **Overcrowded Classrooms:** Many schools, particularly in townships and rural areas, are severely overcrowded, with class sizes far exceeding the recommended student-to-teacher ratio. This makes it difficult for teachers to provide individual attention to students and for students to learn effectively.

- **Lack of Basic Facilities:** Many schools lack essential facilities such as libraries, science labs, and computer rooms. Even when such facilities are present, they are often poorly maintained, further hindering the learning process.

- o **Technology Deficit:** In an increasingly digital world, the lack of access to technology in schools is a critical shortfall. Many students do not have access to computers or the internet, putting them at a significant disadvantage compared to their peers in better-resourced schools.

3. Outdated Curricula

The curricula in South Africa's education system have been slow to evolve and often do not align with the skills required in the modern job market. This mismatch leads to:

- o **Irrelevant Skills:** Many graduates find that the skills they have acquired are not relevant to the needs of employers. This is particularly true in sectors that require technical and vocational skills, which are often overlooked in favour of more traditional academic subjects.

- o **Lack of Emphasis on Vocational Training:** The education system tends to prioritize academic pathways over vocational training, despite the latter being crucial for addressing the skills gap in the economy. As a result, many students are not adequately prepared for the job market.

Impact on Graduate Employability

The challenges within South Africa's education system have a direct and profound impact on the employability of its graduates.

1. **Skills Mismatch**

The disconnect between what is taught in schools and universities and what is needed in the job market results in a significant skills mismatch. Graduates often find that they lack the practical, technical, and soft skills that employers are looking for, making it difficult for them to secure jobs in their fields of study.

2. Low Quality of Education

The overall quality of education, particularly in underfunded and poorly resourced schools, leaves many graduates ill-prepared to compete in a highly competitive job market. Employers are increasingly looking for candidates with strong foundational skills, critical thinking abilities, and the capacity to adapt to new challenges—qualities that many graduates from disadvantaged backgrounds struggle to demonstrate due to the inadequacies of their schooling.

3. Limited Access to Resources

Disparities in access to quality education mean that students from poorer backgrounds are less likely to succeed academically and more likely to struggle to find employment. The lack of access to technology and other resources further exacerbates these challenges, leaving these students at a significant disadvantage in both their education and subsequent job search.

Conclusion

South Africa's education system is in dire need of reform if it is to fulfill its role in preparing young people for the challenges of the 21st century job market. The issues of inadequate funding, poor infrastructure, and outdated curricula are deeply intertwined, creating a cycle that undermines the potential of many young South Africans. Addressing these challenges will require a collaborative effort involving the government, educational institutions, the private sector, and civil society. By tackling the root causes of these systemic issues, there is hope for creating a more effective and equitable education system that truly equips graduates for success in the modern economy.

CHAPTER 2: THE JOB MARKET

South Africa's job market is a complex and often unforgiving landscape, particularly for the country's educated youth. As graduates step out of universities and colleges, many are met not with open doors, but with an overwhelming sense of uncertainty. The job market, once perceived as the next logical step in their journey, quickly reveals itself as a formidable challenge, riddled with obstacles that make finding meaningful employment a daunting task.

Overview of South Africa's Job Market

The South African job market is characterized by a dual economy, with stark contrasts between the formal and informal sectors. The formal sector, where most graduates aim to secure employment, includes industries such as finance, healthcare, education, engineering, and information technology. These sectors typically offer stable employment, benefits, and opportunities for career advancement. However, they are also highly competitive and often require not just qualifications, but also experience and connections that many young graduates lack.

On the other hand, the informal sector, which includes jobs in areas such as street vending, domestic work, and informal trading, is less regulated and offers little in the way of job security or career progression. For many young people, especially those who struggle to break into the formal job market, the informal sector becomes a last resort—a way to make ends meet rather than a stepping stone to a fulfilling career.

In recent years, South Africa has seen a growing number of young people with tertiary qualifications entering a job market that is unable to absorb them. The unemployment rate among young people remains alarmingly high, with those aged 15-34 making up a significant portion of the unemployed population. Even those with degrees and diplomas find themselves in a precarious position, facing intense competition for a limited number of jobs.

Challenges Facing the Job Market

Several key challenges contribute to the difficulties that educated youth face in the South African job market:

1. **High Unemployment**

Unemployment in South Africa is a persistent and deeply entrenched issue, exacerbated by a sluggish economy that has struggled to create enough jobs to meet the demand. The unemployment rate among youth is particularly high, with many young people unable to find work even after completing their education. This situation is further aggravated by the fact that economic growth has been slow and inconsistent, resulting in fewer job opportunities across all sectors.

For young graduates, the high unemployment rate translates into fierce competition for the few available positions. Jobs that once required only a matric certificate now demand a degree, and positions that previously welcomed fresh graduates now prefer candidates with several years of experience. This creates a vicious cycle, where young people are unable to gain the experience they need because they cannot secure a job in the first place.

2. **Skills Mismatch**

The issue of a skills mismatch is another significant barrier to employment for many young South Africans. There is a growing disconnect between the skills that graduates acquire during their studies and the skills that employers actually need. While universities and colleges produce a steady stream of graduates in fields like humanities, social sciences, and business, there is a shortage of qualified candidates in technical fields such as engineering, information technology, and healthcare.

This mismatch is not just a matter of academic focus but also reflects deeper issues within the education system, as discussed in the previous chapter. Many graduates find that their qualifications do not equip them with the practical, job-ready skills that employers are looking for. This leaves them struggling to find work in their chosen fields, often having to settle for jobs outside their areas of expertise, or worse, remaining unemployed.

3. **Nepotism and Networking**

In South Africa, as in many other parts of the world, "who you know" can often be more important than "what you know" when it comes to finding a job. Nepotism and the reliance on personal networks for job opportunities are pervasive issues that disproportionately affect young people who may not have the social connections needed to access job opportunities.

For many graduates, especially those from disadvantaged backgrounds, the lack of a professional network is a significant hurdle. Without the connections that can open doors, they are left to navigate the job market on their own, often without the guidance or support needed to successfully secure employment. This reliance on networks and connections can also perpetuate inequality, as those with established social ties are more likely to find jobs, leaving others behind regardless of their qualifications or capabilities.

Impact on Educated Youth

The challenges within South Africa's job market have a profound impact on the country's educated youth. The inability to secure employment after years of study is not just a professional setback; it is a deeply personal one that affects every aspect of a young person's life.

1. **Economic Strain**

The financial burden of unemployment is severe. Many graduates find themselves unable to repay student loans or support themselves independently. This financial strain often forces them to rely on their families, who may already be struggling, or to take on low-paying, unskilled jobs that do not reflect their education or aspirations.

2. **Emotional and Psychological Toll**

The psychological impact of unemployment cannot be understated. For many young people, the dream of building a career and achieving financial independence is central to their identity and self-worth. When these aspirations are thwarted, it can lead to feelings of inadequacy, anxiety, and depression. The prolonged uncertainty and repeated rejections can erode self-confidence and lead to a sense of hopelessness.

3. **Wasted Potential**

Perhaps the most tragic consequence of this situation is the waste of human potential. South Africa's educated youth represent a valuable resource, full of ideas, energy, and ambition. When they are unable to find meaningful work, their skills and talents go unused, which is not just a personal loss, but a loss for the entire country. The failure to integrate these young people into the workforce has long-term implications for economic growth, social stability, and the country's ability to innovate and compete on a global stage.

Conclusion

The challenges facing South Africa's job market are complex and multifaceted, with high unemployment, skills mismatches, and nepotism creating significant barriers for educated youth. These obstacles not only hinder individual progress but also have broader implications for society as a whole. As the country continues to grapple with these issues, it is essential to find ways to bridge the gap between education and employment, ensuring that the next generation of graduates can contribute meaningfully to the economy and realize their full potential.

CHAPTER 3: THE STRUGGLE IS REAL

The journey from the classroom to the job market is supposed to be one of hope and ambition, but for many of South Africa's educated youth, it is a path fraught with disappointment, frustration, and heartache. In this chapter, we delve into the lived experiences of young graduates who, despite their qualifications and dreams, find themselves grappling with the harsh realities of unemployment. Through their personal stories, we explore the emotional and psychological toll this takes, as well as the coping mechanisms and support systems they rely on to navigate these challenges.

Personal Stories of Educated Unemployed Youth

Behind the statistics and economic reports are real people—young men and women who have invested years of their lives in education, only to find themselves stranded in a job market that has little to offer them. Their stories are as diverse as they are poignant, each one shedding light on the broader issue of youth unemployment in South Africa.

Take Thandi, for example. She graduated at the top of her class with a degree in Environmental Science, full of aspirations to make a difference in the world. She envisioned herself working on projects that would help protect South Africa's natural resources and combat climate change. But after two years of relentless job searching, Thandi finds herself working as a waitress in a local café, far removed from the career she had imagined. Despite her efforts, her qualifications have not translated into employment, leaving her to question the value of the degree she worked so hard to obtain.

Then there's Sipho, who holds a degree in Business Administration. He had dreams of climbing the corporate ladder, but instead, he finds himself sending out hundreds of job applications with little to no response. The few interviews he has secured have ended in disappointment, with employers citing a lack of experience or more qualified candidates as reasons for not hiring him. Sipho's frustration is palpable—he did everything right, followed the prescribed path, yet the opportunities he was promised remain out of reach.

These stories are not isolated incidents; they represent the experiences of countless young South Africans. Each one is a testament to the struggles faced by educated youth in a country where a degree no longer guarantees a job. These individuals are caught in a cycle of applying for positions they are qualified for, only to be told they need experience, and then being unable to gain that experience because they cannot secure employment.

Emotional and Psychological Toll of Unemployment

The impact of unemployment goes far beyond the financial. For many young graduates, the inability to find work is a deeply personal blow that affects their self-esteem, mental health, and overall sense of purpose. The emotional and psychological toll of unemployment is profound, and its effects can be long-lasting.

The initial optimism that accompanies graduation quickly fades as the reality of unemployment sets in. Repeated rejections or, worse, complete silence from potential employers, can erode a person's self-worth. Graduates who once felt confident in their abilities begin to question themselves: Am I not good enough? Did I choose the wrong field? What did I do wrong? These self-doubts can spiral into feelings of inadequacy and failure, making it difficult to maintain motivation.

The stress of prolonged unemployment can also lead to more serious mental health issues, such as anxiety and depression. The uncertainty of the future, coupled with the pressure to meet societal expectations, creates an environment of constant worry and fear. Many young people struggle with feelings of hopelessness, as the path they worked so hard to pave seems to crumble beneath them.

Moreover, the stigma attached to unemployment can exacerbate these emotional challenges. Society often equates success with employment, leading to feelings of shame and embarrassment for those who are unable to find work. This stigma can make it difficult for unemployed graduates to talk about their struggles or seek help, further isolating them in their experiences.

Coping Mechanisms and Support Systems

In the face of such adversity, how do South Africa's educated youth cope? What support systems are available to help them navigate the emotional and psychological challenges of unemployment? The answers vary, but they all highlight the resilience and determination of these young people.

For many, family is the first line of support. Despite the financial strain unemployment places on households, families often provide emotional encouragement and practical assistance, whether it's a place to stay, help with job applications, or simply a listening ear. However, this support can come with its own set of challenges. The pressure to contribute financially or to meet parental expectations can add to the stress, especially when young people feel they are letting their families down.

Friends and peer networks also play a crucial role in coping with unemployment. Sharing experiences with others who are in the same situation can be a source of comfort and solidarity. Peer support groups, both formal and informal, provide a space for young people to vent their frustrations, share job leads, and offer advice to one another. These networks can help alleviate the isolation that often accompanies unemployment, reminding individuals that they are not alone in their struggles.

For some, coping involves finding ways to stay productive and maintain a sense of purpose. Volunteering, freelancing, or pursuing further studies are common strategies employed by unemployed graduates. These activities not only fill the gap left by unemployment but also help to build skills, gain experience, and expand professional networks. They offer a way to remain active and engaged, even when paid employment is elusive.

Mental health services, though not always easily accessible, are another important resource. Counselling and therapy can provide much-needed support for those dealing with the emotional fallout of unemployment. However, the stigma around mental health, coupled with the cost of professional services, means that many young people do not seek the help they need. Addressing this gap is crucial for ensuring that unemployed graduates have access to the care and support that can help them navigate their challenges.

Conclusion

The struggle is indeed real for South Africa's educated unemployed youth. The personal stories of these young people highlight the emotional and psychological toll that unemployment takes, as well as the resilience and resourcefulness they display in coping with their circumstances. While family, friends, and personal initiatives provide some support, there is an urgent need for more comprehensive and accessible support systems. Understanding the human impact of unemployment is essential for addressing the broader issue and finding solutions that not only create jobs but also support the well-being of those who seek them.

CHAPTER 4: SOCIETAL EXPECTATIONS

Societal expectations shape our lives from an early age, guiding our choices, influencing our behavior, and molding our aspirations. For South Africa's educated youth, these expectations often carry a heavy weight, especially in the context of unemployment. This chapter explores the multifaceted pressures that young graduates face from their families, communities, and society at large. We will also examine the stigma attached to unemployment and the profound impact it has on mental health and well-being.

Pressure from Family, Community, and Society

From the moment a child enters school, the expectation is clear: work hard, excel academically, and you will secure a successful future. For many South African families, education is seen as the key to breaking the cycle of poverty and achieving upward mobility. Parents invest their hopes and dreams in their children's education, often making significant sacrifices to ensure they have access to quality schooling and higher education.

This investment, both emotional and financial, creates immense pressure on young people to succeed. Graduating from university is supposed to be the fulfilment of that promise—a ticket to a better life. But when the reality of the job market falls short, and employment is not forthcoming, the burden of unmet expectations can be overwhelming.

Family pressure can be particularly intense. For many young graduates, their parents or guardians have worked tirelessly, sometimes forgoing their own needs, to provide for their education. The expectation is that the graduate will now take on the role of provider, contributing financially to the household and lifting the family out of hardship. When a job does not materialize, the graduate may feel like they have failed not only themselves but also their family. This sense of responsibility can lead to feelings of guilt, shame, and anxiety.

Communities, too, play a role in shaping expectations. In many South African communities, a young person's success is seen as a collective achievement. Neighbours, relatives, and local leaders often take pride in the accomplishments of young graduates, viewing them as role models for others. However, this communal pride can quickly turn into communal pressure. Graduates may feel the weight of their community's expectations, fearing judgment or disappointment if they are unable to secure a job. The pressure to meet these expectations can be suffocating, leading to feelings of isolation and inadequacy.

Society at large also imposes its expectations on young people, often through cultural norms and societal values. Success is frequently equated with employment, financial independence, and material wealth. The societal narrative suggests that education should lead directly to a stable career, a comfortable lifestyle, and upward social mobility. When this narrative does not align with reality, young graduates may struggle with feelings of failure and frustration. They may feel as though they are falling behind their peers or failing to live up to societal standards.

The Stigma of Unemployment

Unemployment carries a significant stigma in many societies, and South Africa is no exception. The stigma is rooted in the belief that one's worth is tied to their ability to contribute economically. When young graduates are unable to find work, they may be perceived as lazy, unmotivated, or undeserving of success. This judgment can come from various sources—family members, friends, neighbours, or even the graduates themselves.

The stigma of unemployment is particularly damaging because it reinforces negative stereotypes and perpetuates a cycle of shame and silence. Graduates who are struggling to find work may be reluctant to talk about their experiences, fearing judgment or ridicule. They may avoid social gatherings, withdraw from their communities, and isolate themselves to avoid the pain of explaining their situation. This isolation can further exacerbate feelings of loneliness and despair.

Moreover, the stigma of unemployment is not just external; it is often internalized by the graduates themselves. When society consistently sends the message that unemployment is a personal failing, young people may begin to believe that they are to blame for their situation. They may feel unworthy of success, question their abilities, and lose confidence in their potential. This internalized stigma can have a devastating impact on their self-esteem and mental health.

Impact on Mental Health and Well-being

The combined pressure from family, community, and society, along with the stigma of unemployment, can take a significant toll on the mental health and well-being of young graduates. The emotional burden of not meeting expectations, coupled with the stress of financial insecurity, can lead to a range of mental health challenges.

Anxiety and depression are common among unemployed graduates. The constant worry about the future, the fear of being judged, and the sense of hopelessness can create a persistent state of anxiety. Graduates may struggle to sleep, experience panic attacks, or feel overwhelmed by even the simplest tasks. Depression can manifest as a deep sense of sadness, a lack of motivation, and a loss of interest in activities that once brought joy. These mental health challenges can make it even more difficult for graduates to seek employment or engage with their communities.

The impact on mental health is further compounded by the lack of adequate support systems. Mental health services in South Africa are often inaccessible or stigmatized, leaving many young people without the help they need. Those who do seek help may face long wait times, high costs, or a lack of understanding from healthcare providers. As a result, many graduates are left to cope with their struggles on their own, relying on unhealthy coping mechanisms such as substance abuse, withdrawal, or denial.

The long-term effects of unemployment on mental health can be profound. Prolonged periods of unemployment can lead to chronic stress, which has been linked to a range of physical and mental health problems, including heart disease, weakened immune function, and cognitive decline. The psychological impact of unemployment can also affect future job prospects, as graduates may struggle with confidence and self-esteem when applying for jobs or during interviews.

Conclusion

The societal expectations placed on South Africa's educated youth are significant, and the pressure to meet these expectations can be overwhelming. When young graduates are unable to secure employment, they face not only the practical challenges of financial insecurity but also the emotional and psychological burden of unmet expectations and societal stigma. The impact on their mental health and well-being is profound, highlighting the need for more compassionate and supportive approaches to addressing youth unemployment.

Understanding the human impact of societal expectations and unemployment is crucial for developing effective solutions. It is not enough to create jobs; we must also create a society that values and supports its young people, regardless of their employment status. By addressing the stigma of unemployment, providing accessible mental health support, and fostering a culture of empathy and understanding, we can help South Africa's educated youth navigate the challenges they face and build a future where they can thrive.

CHAPTER 5: GOVERNMENT INITIATIVES

The South African government has long recognized the importance of addressing youth unemployment, particularly among the educated. In response to the growing crisis, numerous programs and initiatives have been introduced over the years, aimed at bridging the gap between education and employment. This chapter delves into these government efforts, critically examining their effectiveness, accessibility, and sustainability, while also offering recommendations for improvement.

Overview of Government Programs and Initiatives

The South African government has implemented several initiatives to combat youth unemployment, each with the goal of providing young people with the skills, experience, and opportunities needed to secure meaningful employment. These initiatives range from large-scale national programs to smaller, targeted interventions, each designed to address specific aspects of the unemployment crisis.

One of the most prominent government programs is the **Youth Employment Service (YES)**, launched in 2018. This initiative aims to create one million work opportunities for young South Africans by partnering with the private sector. Through YES, businesses are incentivized to provide young people with work experience, mentorship, and training, helping them to build the skills and networks necessary to enter the job market.

Another key initiative is the **National Youth Development Agency (NYDA)**, which offers a variety of services to young people, including career guidance, skills development, and entrepreneurship support. The NYDA also provides funding for youth-owned businesses, helping young entrepreneurs to start and grow their enterprises, thus creating jobs for themselves and others.

The **Skills Development Act** and the **National Skills Fund (NSF)** are also central to the government's efforts to address youth unemployment. These programs focus on providing vocational training and upskilling opportunities to young people, particularly those from disadvantaged backgrounds. The goal is to equip them with the practical skills needed to meet the demands of the job market.

In addition to these national programs, there are numerous regional and sector-specific initiatives, such as **artisan training programs**, **learnerships**, and **internships**, all aimed at enhancing the employability of young South Africans. These programs often involve partnerships between the government, educational institutions, and industry stakeholders, reflecting a collaborative approach to tackling unemployment.

Critique: Effectiveness, Accessibility, and Sustainability

While these government initiatives represent significant efforts to address youth unemployment, their effectiveness, accessibility, and sustainability have been subject to considerable debate. Many young South Africans, particularly those who are educated, continue to struggle to find work, raising questions about the impact of these programs.

Effectiveness: One of the primary criticisms of government initiatives is their limited impact on the overall unemployment rate. Despite the introduction of programs like YES and NYDA, the unemployment rate among educated youth remains stubbornly high. Critics argue that while these initiatives have created opportunities for some, they have not been able to address the structural issues that underpin the unemployment crisis, such as the skills mismatch between education and the job market, and the slow pace of economic growth.

Furthermore, the quality of the jobs created by these initiatives is often called into question. Many of the opportunities provided are short-term, low-paying, or do not align with the qualifications and aspirations of young graduates. As a result, while these programs may provide temporary relief, they do not necessarily lead to long-term, sustainable employment.

Accessibility: Accessibility is another significant challenge. While government programs are theoretically available to all young South Africans, in practice, many face barriers to participation. These barriers can include a lack of information about available opportunities, bureaucratic hurdles, and geographical constraints, particularly for those living in rural or underserved areas. Additionally, there is often a lack of support for young people during the application process, making it difficult for those who need these programs the most to access them.

For example, the process of applying for funding through the NYDA or securing a placement through YES can be complex and time-consuming, deterring many young people from participating. There are also concerns that these programs are not adequately reaching those from disadvantaged backgrounds, who may lack the resources or networks to navigate the system effectively.

Sustainability: The sustainability of government initiatives is another area of concern. Many programs rely heavily on government funding, which can be subject to budget cuts or shifting political priorities. This dependency on public funding raises questions about the long-term viability of these initiatives, particularly in a context of economic uncertainty and fiscal constraints.

Moreover, some programs are criticized for being too narrowly focused or short-sighted, addressing the symptoms of unemployment rather than the root causes. For example, while initiatives like YES provide valuable work experience, they do not necessarily address the broader economic and structural issues that contribute to high unemployment, such as the lack of job creation in key sectors or the inadequacy of the education system.

Recommendations for Improvement

To enhance the effectiveness, accessibility, and sustainability of government initiatives, several key changes are needed. These recommendations are aimed at creating a more inclusive, impactful, and resilient approach to addressing youth unemployment.

1. **Align Education with Market Needs:** One of the most critical steps is to ensure that the education system is better aligned with the needs of the job market. This includes updating curricula to reflect current industry demands, expanding vocational training and apprenticeship programs, and fostering

stronger partnerships between educational institutions and the private sector. By equipping young people with the skills that employers are actively seeking, the gap between education and employment can be narrowed.

2. **Enhance Accessibility:** Improving access to government programs is essential to ensuring that all young people, regardless of their background or location, can benefit from these initiatives. This could involve simplifying application processes, increasing outreach and awareness efforts, and providing targeted support to those from disadvantaged communities. Additionally, leveraging technology to create more accessible platforms for information and application could help bridge the gap for those in rural or underserved areas.

3. **Focus on Quality and Sustainability:** To create long-term, sustainable employment,

government initiatives must prioritize quality over quantity. This means focusing on creating meaningful, well-paying jobs that align with the qualifications and aspirations of young graduates. It also involves ensuring that these programs are not solely dependent on government funding, but are supported by partnerships with the private sector and civil society.

4. **Address Structural Issues:** Finally, it is crucial to address the broader structural issues that contribute to youth unemployment. This includes implementing policies that promote economic growth and job creation, particularly in high-potential sectors such as technology, renewable energy, and tourism. It also involves tackling issues such as corruption, nepotism, and inequality, which undermine the effectiveness of government initiatives and perpetuate the cycle of unemployment.

Conclusion

Government initiatives play a vital role in addressing youth unemployment in South Africa, but there is still much work to be done to ensure their effectiveness, accessibility, and sustainability. By critically examining these programs and implementing the recommended changes, there is hope for a more inclusive and prosperous future for South Africa's educated youth. The government, together with educational institutions, the private sector, and civil society, must work collaboratively to create an environment where all young people have the opportunity to succeed.

CHAPTER 6: ENTREPRENEURSHIP AND INNOVATION

In the face of high unemployment rates, particularly among educated youth, entrepreneurship and innovation have emerged as powerful tools for creating opportunities and driving economic growth. This chapter explores the potential of entrepreneurship and innovation in South Africa, the challenges that young entrepreneurs face, and the inspiring success stories that demonstrate the resilience and creativity of South Africa's youth.

Opportunities for Entrepreneurship and Innovation

In recent years, entrepreneurship has gained significant attention as a viable solution to unemployment. The idea is simple yet powerful: if jobs are not available, young people can create their own. South Africa, with its diverse economy and growing middle class, offers a range of opportunities for aspiring entrepreneurs. From technology start-ups to social enterprises, the possibilities are vast and varied.

One of the most promising areas for entrepreneurship in South Africa is the technology sector. With the rise of digital platforms and the increasing penetration of the internet, there is a growing demand for tech-based solutions that address local challenges. Young entrepreneurs are leveraging technology to create innovative products and services that cater to the unique needs of South African consumers. For example, mobile apps that facilitate financial inclusion, e-commerce platforms that support small businesses, and digital learning tools that enhance education are just a few examples of how technology is driving entrepreneurship.

Another area ripe for innovation is the green economy. As the world grapples with the effects of climate change, there is a growing need for sustainable solutions that reduce environmental impact. South Africa, with its abundant natural resources and commitment to renewable energy, offers significant opportunities for green entrepreneurs. Whether it's developing renewable energy solutions, promoting sustainable agriculture, or creating eco-friendly products, young entrepreneurs are finding ways to contribute to a more sustainable future while building profitable businesses.

Social entrepreneurship is also gaining traction in South Africa, as young people seek to address social challenges while creating economic value. These entrepreneurs are driven by a desire to make a positive impact on their communities, whether it's through providing access to education, healthcare, or clean water. Social enterprises are not only creating jobs but are also addressing some of the most pressing issues facing South Africa today.

Challenges: Funding, Mentorship, and Market Access

While the opportunities for entrepreneurship are plentiful, the journey is not without its challenges. For many young South Africans, the path to entrepreneurship is fraught with obstacles that can be difficult to overcome.

Funding is one of the most significant challenges facing young entrepreneurs. Access to capital is crucial for starting and growing a business, yet many young people struggle to secure the funding they need. Traditional financial institutions often view young entrepreneurs as high-risk, particularly those without a track record or collateral. This lack of access to credit can stifle innovation and prevent promising ideas from reaching their full potential. While there are government programs and private initiatives aimed at providing funding to young entrepreneurs, these are often insufficient to meet the demand.

Mentorship is another critical challenge. Entrepreneurship can be a lonely and daunting journey, particularly for those who are just starting out. Having access to experienced mentors who can provide guidance, advice, and support can make a significant difference in the success of a young entrepreneur. However, mentorship opportunities are not always readily available, particularly in underserved communities. The lack of mentorship can lead to mistakes, missed opportunities, and ultimately, business failure.

Market access is another hurdle that young entrepreneurs must navigate. Even the most innovative product or service can fail if it doesn't reach the right market. For young entrepreneurs, breaking into established markets or reaching new customers can be a daunting task. This is particularly true for those operating in industries that are dominated by large, established players. Additionally, navigating the complexities of supply chains, distribution networks, and marketing can be overwhelming for those who lack experience or resources.

Success Stories and Case Studies

Despite these challenges, many young South Africans have managed to overcome the odds and build successful businesses. Their stories serve as a source of inspiration and a testament to the resilience and creativity of South Africa's youth.

One such success story is that of **Thato Kgatlhanye**, the founder of Rethaka, a company that produces school bags made from recycled plastic. These innovative bags have a built-in solar panel that charges during the day and provides light for children to study at night. Thato's journey began when she noticed the challenges faced by children in rural areas who didn't have access to electricity. With limited resources, she started a small business that not only addressed this issue but also contributed to environmental sustainability. Today, Rethaka is a thriving social enterprise that has garnered international recognition and created jobs for many young people in her community.

Another inspiring example is **Ludwick Marishane**, the inventor of DryBath, a waterless bathing solution that allows people to clean themselves without using water. Ludwick came up with the idea while still in high school, after seeing the challenges faced by people in water-scarce areas. With determination and perseverance, he developed the product and turned it into a successful business. Today, DryBath is used in various settings, from rural communities to disaster relief efforts, and has earned Ludwick numerous accolades, including being named one of TIME magazine's "Top 30 Under 30" entrepreneurs.

These stories, among many others, highlight the potential of young South Africans to drive change and create innovative solutions to the challenges they face. They demonstrate that, with the right support and resources, young entrepreneurs can overcome obstacles and build businesses that make a difference.

Conclusion

Entrepreneurship and innovation hold the key to unlocking the potential of South Africa's educated youth. While the challenges are significant, the opportunities are vast, and the success stories of young entrepreneurs across the country are a testament to what is possible. By addressing the barriers to funding, mentorship, and market access, and by fostering a supportive ecosystem for entrepreneurship, South Africa can empower its youth to take control of their futures and contribute to the country's economic and social development.

In the end, the journey of entrepreneurship is not just about creating jobs; it's about building a culture of innovation, resilience, and self-reliance. It's about young people taking the lead in shaping their own destinies and, in the process, creating a brighter future for themselves and their communities. The stories in this chapter remind us that while the struggle is real, so too is the potential for success. With the right support, South Africa's youth can rise to the challenge and turn their degrees of despair into degrees of opportunity.

CHAPTER 7: BREAKING THE CYCLE

The challenges faced by South Africa's educated, unemployed youth are deep-rooted and multifaceted. While the issues may seem overwhelming, there is hope for change. This chapter explores strategies for breaking the cycle of unemployment and despair, focusing on the critical areas of education reform, job creation, and social support. It also highlights the roles that individuals, communities, and organizations can play in driving this change, concluding with a call to action for all stakeholders.

Strategies for Change: Education Reform, Job Creation, and Social Support

Education Reform

To break the cycle of unemployment, South Africa's education system must undergo significant reform. The current system, while expansive, often fails to equip students with the skills and knowledge needed in the modern job market. Education reform must begin with a re-evaluation of curricula to ensure that they are aligned with the demands of the economy. This means placing a greater emphasis on STEM (Science, Technology, Engineering, and Mathematics) education, as well as vocational training that provides practical skills.

Reforming education also involves improving the quality of teaching and learning environments. Teachers must be better supported through professional development and training, ensuring they can deliver relevant and engaging content. Additionally, schools and universities need to be equipped with the resources necessary to foster innovation and critical thinking, from modern technology to well-maintained facilities.

Another crucial aspect of education reform is making higher education more accessible and affordable. The financial barriers that prevent many talented young South Africans from pursuing tertiary education must be addressed. This can be achieved through increased funding for scholarships, bursaries, and student loans, as well as initiatives that reduce the overall cost of education. By making education more inclusive, we can ensure that more young people are prepared for the challenges of the job market.

Job Creation

Education reform alone is not enough; there must also be a concerted effort to create jobs that match the skills of graduates. Job creation is a complex challenge that requires collaboration between the government, private sector, and civil society. One key strategy is to promote industries that have the potential to absorb large numbers of educated youth, such as technology, renewable energy, and healthcare.

The government can play a pivotal role in job creation by implementing policies that encourage entrepreneurship and investment in key sectors. This includes reducing bureaucratic red tape, providing tax incentives for businesses that hire young graduates, and investing in infrastructure projects that create jobs. Additionally, public-private partnerships can be instrumental in driving job creation, particularly in sectors that require significant capital investment.

Another important aspect of job creation is addressing the skills mismatch that plagues many graduates. This can be achieved by fostering closer collaboration between educational institutions and industry to ensure that curricula are aligned with the needs of employers. Internship programs, apprenticeships, and work-integrated learning opportunities can help bridge the gap between education and employment, providing students with the practical experience they need to succeed in the job market.

Social Support

Breaking the cycle of unemployment also requires a robust social support system that helps young people navigate the challenges they face. This includes not only financial assistance but also mental health support, career counselling, and mentoring programs. Unemployment can take a significant emotional and psychological toll, leading to feelings of despair, anxiety, and worthlessness. Providing accessible mental health services is crucial in helping young people cope with the pressures of unemployment and stay motivated in their job search.

Career counselling and mentoring programs can provide invaluable guidance and support to young graduates as they navigate the job market. Mentors can offer advice on career choices, help with job applications, and provide networking opportunities that can open doors to employment. Additionally, community-based organizations can play a vital role in providing social support, offering safe spaces where young people can share their experiences, build resilience, and develop the skills needed to overcome the challenges they face.

Role of Individuals, Communities, and Organizations

Individuals

Each individual has a role to play in breaking the cycle of unemployment. For young graduates, this means taking proactive steps to improve their employability, such as seeking out internships, volunteering, and continuously learning new skills. It also involves being resilient and adaptable, recognizing that the path to success may not be straightforward, and being open to exploring alternative career paths.

For educators, policymakers, and business leaders, the responsibility lies in creating environments that support the development and employment of young people. This includes advocating for education reform, investing in job creation initiatives, and mentoring the next generation of leaders. By taking ownership of these challenges, individuals can contribute to a broader movement for change.

Communities

Communities play a critical role in supporting young people and creating opportunities for them to thrive. Local communities can develop initiatives that provide young people with the skills, resources, and networks they need to succeed. This might include community-based training programs, entrepreneurship hubs, and support groups that offer guidance and encouragement.

Moreover, communities can work together to challenge the stigma associated with unemployment, fostering an environment of support rather than judgment. By coming together to address the issue of youth unemployment, communities can create a collective impact that drives real change.

Organizations

Organizations, both public and private, have a significant role to play in breaking the cycle of unemployment. Companies can invest in youth by offering internships, apprenticeships, and entry-level positions that provide valuable work experience. They can also engage in corporate social responsibility initiatives that focus on education, job creation, and entrepreneurship.

Non-governmental organizations (NGOs) and community-based organizations can also contribute by providing essential services such as career counselling, mentorship, and job placement assistance. These organizations can act as bridges between young people and the job market, helping to connect them with opportunities that align with their skills and aspirations.

Call to Action

The time to act is now. South Africa's youth unemployment crisis is not just a problem for the young people affected; it is a national crisis that requires urgent and sustained action from all sectors of society. Breaking the cycle of unemployment will require a coordinated effort, with contributions from individuals, communities, organizations, and the government.

This chapter calls on educators to push for reforms that better prepare students for the realities of the job market. It calls on businesses to invest in the potential of young people, offering them the opportunities they need to succeed. It calls on communities to support their young members, creating environments where they can thrive. And it calls on the government to take bold steps to create jobs, support education reform, and provide the social support necessary to help young people navigate the challenges they face.

The future of South Africa depends on its youth. By working together to break the cycle of unemployment, we can create a society where every young person has the opportunity to fulfil their potential, contribute to the economy, and build a brighter future for themselves and the nation. Let this chapter be a reminder that while the challenges are great, the power to change the narrative lies within us all.

CHAPTER 8: THE PATH FORWARD

As we reach the conclusion of "Degrees of Despair: The Struggle of South Africa's Educated Unemployed Youth," it is essential to reflect on the journey we've taken through the challenges, complexities, and heartaches faced by the country's educated youth. This chapter synthesizes the key findings from our exploration, reflects on the way forward, and offers a message of hope and resilience for a generation that has endured much but has the potential to rise above adversity.

Summary of Key Findings

Our journey began with an in-depth look at South Africa's education system, revealing a structure that, despite its intentions, often falls short of equipping young people with the skills and knowledge they need to succeed in a competitive job market. We examined how inadequate funding, poor infrastructure, and outdated curricula contribute to a significant mismatch between the skills graduates possess and the demands of the labour market. This gap leaves many young South Africans struggling to find employment that matches their qualifications and aspirations.

In exploring the job market, we uncovered the harsh realities faced by educated youth: high unemployment rates, systemic issues such as nepotism, and a saturated market that offers limited opportunities. The stories shared in these chapters are not just statistics but real-life experiences of frustration, disappointment, and shattered dreams. These narratives paint a vivid picture of the emotional and psychological toll that unemployment takes on young people, affecting their self-worth, mental health, and overall well-being.

The societal pressures that weigh heavily on the unemployed youth were also brought to light, illustrating how expectations from family, community, and society can exacerbate the stigma of joblessness. This stigma often leads to feelings of isolation, shame, and despair, further compounding the challenges faced by young people who are already struggling to navigate an unforgiving job market.

We also examined government initiatives aimed at addressing youth unemployment, finding that while efforts have been made, there is still much work to be done. The effectiveness, accessibility, and sustainability of these programs have been called into question, with many young people finding them inadequate or out of reach. Our analysis highlighted the need for more targeted, innovative, and inclusive approaches to tackling the unemployment crisis.

In our discussion of entrepreneurship and innovation, we identified both opportunities and obstacles. While entrepreneurship offers a promising avenue for job creation and economic empowerment, challenges such as limited access to funding, mentorship, and market opportunities hinder the ability of young entrepreneurs to succeed. Nevertheless, the success stories and case studies presented in this book demonstrate that with the right support and resources, South Africa's youth have the potential to drive meaningful change and contribute to the country's economic growth.

Finally, in the chapter on breaking the cycle, we outlined a comprehensive strategy for addressing the root causes of youth unemployment. Education reform, job creation, and social support are critical components of this strategy, with a call for collaboration between government, industry, educational institutions, and communities. The role of individuals, organizations, and society as a whole in fostering change was emphasized, underscoring the collective responsibility we all share in building a better future for South Africa's youth.

Reflections on the Way Forward

As we look to the future, it is clear that addressing youth unemployment in South Africa requires a multifaceted approach. Systemic change is needed at every level, from education to employment. The solutions must be holistic, targeting not just the symptoms but the root causes of the crisis.

Education reform is essential. We must rethink what and how we teach, ensuring that curricula are relevant and responsive to the needs of a rapidly changing world. But education alone is not enough. We must also focus on creating jobs, particularly in sectors that have the potential for growth and innovation. This requires investment, policy changes, and a commitment to fostering entrepreneurship and innovation.

Social support systems must be strengthened to provide a safety net for those who are unemployed. Mental health support, career counselling, and mentorship programs are vital in helping young people navigate the challenges of joblessness and maintain their resilience.

But beyond these structural changes, we must also foster a cultural shift—one that values every individual's potential, regardless of their employment status. Society must move away from stigmatizing the unemployed and instead recognize the systemic barriers that many face. By doing so, we can create a more inclusive, supportive environment where young people are encouraged to pursue their dreams and contribute to the nation's future.

Hope and Resilience in the Face of Despair

Despite the challenges we have explored in this book, there is a thread of hope that runs through the stories, the struggles, and the potential solutions. South Africa's youth are resilient, resourceful, and determined. They are not passive victims of their circumstances but are actively seeking ways to overcome the obstacles in their path.

This book is not just a diagnosis of the problem but a call to action. It is a plea for policymakers, educators, employers, and society as a whole to recognize the urgency of this issue and to work towards sustainable solutions. The future of South Africa depends on its youth, and it is imperative that they are given the opportunities to succeed.

As we conclude, let us carry forward the stories of struggle with a renewed sense of purpose. Let us be inspired by the resilience of the young men and women who, despite facing overwhelming odds, continue to strive for a better future. Their strength and determination are a testament to the unyielding spirit that, with the right support and opportunities, can overcome even the most daunting challenges.

The road ahead may be long, but it is not without hope. Together, we can build a future where every young South African has the chance to realize their potential, contribute to society, and live with dignity and purpose. This is the vision that *Degrees of Despair* seeks to inspire—a vision of a South Africa where despair gives way to hope, and where the dreams of its youth are not only realized but celebrated.

CAN I ASK A FAVOUR?

If you enjoyed this book, found it useful or otherwise then I'd really appreciate it if you would post a short review on Amazon. I do read all the reviews personally so that I can continually write what people are wanting.

Thanks for your support!